The Life Of An Enclosed Nun: By A Mother Superior...

Life

The Author

Frontispiece—"The Enclosed Nun."

The Life of
An Enclosed Nun

By

A Mother Superior

With a frontispiece portrait

New York: The John Lane Company

London: A. C. Fifield

1911

Contents

Publisher's Note

By the author's wish certain alterations have been made in the frontispiece and text of this book, in order to prevent identification of herself or her Order. A few simplifications and explanations have also been necessary, as it was desired that the book should be comprehensible to non-Catholics.

"The Mother House! the Convent home!
    Blest home of peace and prayer and praise;
Sweet shrine of vowed and virgin hearts,
    God's own through consecrated days.

All day their dove-like thoughts take wing,
    Seeking the Eucharistic shrine;
Here lily-like love, grace-lit, blooms
    In brides of Christ, the Spouse Divine.

Loved sanctuary of the soul,
    Swept of all worldly dust and dross,
Lit with His light, the Kindly Light,
    Sweet with the shadow of the Cross.

And here the white, adoring hours
    Shall pass, all souls in sweet accord,
Like acolytes with fragrant flowers,
    Surpliced and singing to the Lord."

                    From *The Universe.*

The
Life of an Enclosed Nun

Chapter I

At School

IN the year 1883, I being then sixteen years of age, my mother decided to send me to a convent school near Brussels in order that I might learn French and fit myself to become a teacher. We were not Catholics, but we were a family of five girls, and my father was only a struggling doctor, and it was obvious we should have to earn our own livings. My eldest sister had gone to the London Hospital to learn nursing; if I remember aright a new matron had just been appointed

there who was trying to get ladies to come and work in the wards; my second sister was nursery governess to some children who lived near us, but neither of these two seemed to have prospects of ever succeeding well in life. So my mother, having heard of this very cheap school — £30 for twelve months—decided I must go; but she admonished me beforehand not to become an idolater or believer in the Pope. I hated the thought of the school, for I loved the haphazard of our untidy, unpunctual home, and I especially appreciated my free Sundays, when I roamed about London listening to teachers and preachers of all sorts. Moncure Conway at South Place was a great admiration of mine then, but I also remember hearing Jowett at Westminster Abbey that year, and also hearing Gladstone read the lessons at some church in Holborn. We were all supposed to be members of the Church of England, and mother always went to a Sunday service at the church nearest us ; but, frankly, we were all agnostics. I had been confirmed when only twelve because my two elder sisters were going to be confirmed, and it was thought better we should " all get it over together."

In just the same way, when my sister Nellie had measles, we were all put into the same room with her that we might catch them. In an impecunious family of five daughters there is small room for individuality.

So I wept and implored to be allowed to study science instead of French ; but it was no use, and one sad day in September I found myself sitting on the deck of a steamer, one of a circle of a dozen girls surrounding a black-robed nun. Sœur Marthe told us stories and chatted brightly, trying to make the nervous ones forget the sea ; but it was a cold and dreary journey, and the end to me was more terrible than aught I had imagined.

How shall I rightly recall my horror at the huge dormitory and its curtain-less beds ? The two washing taps over the tiny basins, and the total absence of all privacy ; and, it seemed to me, cleanliness. Then the girls wore uni-form black pinafores and little black capes, and all over thirteen had to wear their hair twisted up behind in a single plait. There were some eighty girls in the school, of whom only twelve were English, and the English were carefully kept apart from one another, to prevent them speaking their own language and force them to speak French. Then the food was a great trial—coffee and rolls for breakfast, and for *déjeuner* huge bowls of greasy soup with lumps of bread floating in it. I could laugh now to so describe these things, but I am trying to give my impressions of the time. I was intensely English and opinionated, and full of furious disgust with all and everyone. The girls were nincompoops, and the nuns were fools. How could you play with girls who couldn't catch a ball ? And how could you work with nuns who had never heard of Huxley ? Such was my attitude, and for many weeks my misery was extreme ; but I was very reserved and few guessed what I suffered. Then, of course, the inevitable happened ; I gradually discovered that some of the girls were quite nice—"jolly," I think was the term I should then have used ; and that some of the nuns were quite clever. Sœur Marthe was the head of the school, and when I found out she was a splendid Latin scholar, and an enthusiast in mathematics, my opinion that all speakers of French were idiots slowly changed. True Sœur Marthe astonished me very much by her blazing eyes, as after demonstrating some mathematical problem she cried: "Always three! The inevitable three!"

But still, euclid and algebra were sensible things I wished to know; these were things every English boy was taught; these were subjects that would be useful to me, if ever I won to my then heart's desire—a university education!

We English girls were marched off every Sunday morning to the Protestant church, where a pastor in a black gown gave us an hour's denunciation in French. He often aimed his sermons at us, and at our wickedness in being in a Catholic school simply because it was cheap; luckily, in my first days of misery I did not understand him well enough to appreciate this injustice. We were not allowed to enter the convent chapel without permission from our parents, and the nuns never spoke to us about religion. But the

other girls did! And as that first
Christmas came near the great ques-
tion of discussion amongst the girls
was, who was to be allowed to go to
the midnight mass ? By this time my
curiosity was fairly aroused as to the
Catholic religion ; the air of mystery
that surrounded the chapel and the
nuns' wing, the dreadful whispers about
fastings, and confessions, and penances
that one heard from the girls very
naturally appealed to my inquisitive-
ness—but to nothing else. I was the
rankest little materialist, and wrapped
up in self-complacency and conceit.
However, I wrote home and asked my
mother to send out a permit for me to
attend the convent chapel when I desired, and I drew such a lively picture
of the dreariness of the Protestant
church that my mother acceded. Then
I applied for permission to attend the
midnight mass, and owing to my age,
nearly seventeen, it was granted.

There had been great preparations for Christmas—a few of the girls had gone home, but not many; several more were going for the New Year; but the school as a whole was one where girls resided all the year round. There was the decoration of the chapel and the going to confession on Christmas Eve—in which I had no share. Then at eight o'clock we were all sent to bed, and no sooner had I fallen asleep than it seemed to me a voice whispered in my ear: "C'est onze-heure et demi : levez toi."

I struggled out of bed, and there up and down the silent dormitory were girls hastily slipping on their garments, then falling on their knees for a brief prayer and passing down to the chapel. Speech was not allowed in the dormitories. I hurried down and found two long lines of white-veiled girls drawn up in the refectory; the nun in charge eyed me and the other

Protestant girls who came sleepily down with obvious disfavour. She sent us back to fetch our hats and then took us round out of doors to what was called the " secular " end of the chapel, without the grill, and left us there in darkness and alone.

The chapel was small but very richly ornamented, and all round the altar was brilliantly alight. We were at the very back and had no lights. Presently the door on the east, which was reached by a covered corridor from the convent, opened and the schoolgirls came in two by two, touching their fingers in the holy-water stoup, and crossing themselves as they entered. Then they knelt and bowed low before the altar, and so passed to their seats. Were these white-robed, reverent maidens the rather vicious and noisy girls of the school ? Then, two by two, the nuns filed in, then the little servant girls ; and all was in silence. Then

B

three priests and two acolytes entered and the organ broke forth and the mass began. I am not musical, but still the beauty of the music and the sweet voices of the nuns stirred my heart, and when, to the old familiar tune, the *Adeste Fideles* began, I murmured the words in English and longed, longed for a " mass-book " that I might follow it in Latin. I reckon my conversion began at the singing of the *Adeste ;* and I know that many and many a convert has been won to Holy Church by the midnight mass. The extraordinary reverence of the nuns as they went up with folded hands and downcast eyes ; all that symbolic genuflexion and movement ; all the wondrous roll of Latin, absorbed and excited me. Here was a world of which I knew nothing. Next morning I borrowed a missal from one of the girls and set myself to study the Latin that was used. I was bewildered

to find the Nicene Creed, the Lord's
Prayer, and so few references to Our
Lady and the Saints. I had regarded
Catholics as differing in all essentials
from Protestants. I asked one of the
girls why there were three masses for
Christmas Day, and she answered
roughly for the three births of Christ—
the midnight mass to represent the
birth away back in the black womb
of time ; the second or dawn mass to
represent the birth of Christ on earth ;
the third full daylight mass to represent the birth of Christ in the heart.
Think of my materialistic little wooden
head run up against such thoughts as
the three births of Christ ! Then
another girl lent me an English copy
of " The Key of Heaven," where I
came across the Litany of the Blessed
Virgin :—

"Mystical Rose,
Tower of David,
House of Gold."

Such expressions bewildered and shocked me, I knew not why.

I suppose I must try and put down one or two other memories of what impressed me in those old days. One morning when we were dressing in our cold, dark dormitories someone upset a candle and set fire to a bed. I flew to the nuns' refectory shouting, " Help, help ! " then suddenly stopped, as I found myself in the long, dark room. A narrow trestle table stretched down the room and on it were two candles and some twenty rolls of bread—each placed about four feet apart. Opposite each roll stood a nun, silent, hands clasped. Under a huge crucifix at the top of the table stood the shrivelled up little old " Mère Supérieure "— scarcely ever seen of the schoolgirls. Her burning eyes shot down on me and stilled me ; with a slight wave of the hand she motioned to Sœur Marthe, who silently slipped out of her place

and glided down and led me away.
And as we went I heard the weak
voice of the Rev. Mother go on with
the lengthy Latin grace. Not another
nun moved. And there was only bread
on the table—no coffee! And there
were no seats. As I got to know of
the hardships of the nuns, the poor
food and poor accommodation for the
girls seemed to me as nothing.

Towards the end of my first year I
wrote home and asked permission to
stay for a second. This was granted.
During this second year Sœur Marthe
was taken ill; when she was dying I
begged earnestly to be allowed to go
and see her, and got permission. I
never before had seen anything so
poor and simple as her cell—and to
see her lying there in her stiff cap and
veil and heavy robe seemed so horribly
uncomfortable and unkind. As I came
away from her cell I looked in at the
open doors of some of the other cells I

passed, and in some were crowds of tawdry pictures and old books, and there were shawls and rugs and a general atmosphere of personal possessions. And I felt somehow that Sœur Marthe, with her walls bare but for the crucifix, and no furniture but her bed, her chair, and her *prie-dieu*, was nearer perfection. That little glimpse of Sœur Marthe in her cell remained with me as a mental picture for many a long day.

Chapter II

Conversion

AS the time to return home grew near I got very excited and happy; all home things had taken a rosy aspect, and particularly I longed to talk over many subjects with my father. I had a vast reverence for his intellectual powers, and his kindness and patience were always unbounded. But home proved to be far more shabby and disorderly than I had remembered it, and the constant noise and worry and want of system jarred on my nerves. I did not find the affection and sympathy I expected, and I felt more horribly alone than ever in my life before.

I got a post as governess to two

girls only a little younger than myself, but in much better circumstances, and on the whole I suppose I got some enjoyment out of the winter. It was a remarkably cold winter—1885-6—and there was lots of skating, and many sledges to be seen in the park. There was a wonderful exhibition of Millais's pictures, including the " Vale of Rest " —the two nuns sitting by the grave ; it carried my thoughts back to Sœur Marthe. My pupils were nice, lively girls, and I went skating and sledging with them, and to some theatres and dances. I tried eagerly to amuse myself, but the more I tried the more wretched I got. On Sundays I wandered from church to church, and it was all as sawdust in my mouth. I passed the Carmelite Church and the Oratory again and again—but I would not go in. I tried timidly to get my father to speak about religion, but he was not encouraging. " There isn't a ha'penny to choose between them, my dear; they're all founded on lies. Just follow the convention of the country you're in, for it probably fits the climate. That's why you shouldn't be a Roman Catholic in England; it's too cold and damp here for fasting. We need our English beef, though the Italians can live on macaroni."

Small things were constantly swaying me. I read Newman's " Apologia," I read an interview with Miss Mary Anderson, and was astonished to learn that the beautiful actress was a Catholic; and then I fell in with a ritualistic curate. I went to his church, and with my knowledge of the real Catholic services, this imitation seemed a hollow mockery. I was, in fact, craving for the mass, but yet fighting vigorously against myself. I told myself that I did not believe in the Resurrection, I did not believe in the supernatural, and that as for believing in all the Saints and all the miracles of the Roman Church it was a sheer impossibility.

Then I drifted into a little slummy Catholic church that shall be nameless, and heard a dear old priest thundering crude dogma at his Irish flock, in a way that almost made me sick. I thought his religion was more materialistic than my agnosticism. And yet a certain fascination took me back again and again. He was so very sure ! At last one day I spoke to him, and in a minute we were arguing hotly over the " blessed martyrs "—I counting up those burnt by Queen Mary, and he counting up those killed by Henry VIII and Elizabeth. This led to my reading up the religious history of that period in the British Museum, and waiting every Sunday after mass for Father F. to pour out on him my freshly acquired knowledge. But he was Irish and made of indiarubber ;

you couldn't squash him! If you pressed him down in one place, he only bulged out in another!

" An' did ye notice that nice little bit in ' God's Judgment on the Black Friars,' about the priest that was so sorry his young nephew was taken and he left, and the very next day as he sailed down the Thames the boat struck against the bridge and God took him too. Written by one of yer own Protestants that pamphlet was, and sure, I never saw the Faith shine brighter to those that had eyes to see ! "

I could not help it ; I asked Father F. to receive me into the Church—I had no idea of what I was proposing. I can laugh and rejoice now in looking back on that time ! I was months and months " under instruction," going to Father F. twice a week.

Not one jot or tittle would he abate for me, and this was the sort of thing that went on evening after evening :

"Do ye believe in the Real Presence ? "

" Yes, Father."

" And why do ye believe in it ? "

" Because Holy Church says so."

" And is that the reason ye are going to give yer Protestant friends ? Have ye not even learnt yer penny Catechism yet ? Take this book and away home wi' ye ; ye will learn by heart the passages marked in pencil, and ye will read the whole of this Chapter VI, and be ready to answer questions on the same, before ye come to me again."

I am sure no schoolboy ever shed more tears over the third book of Euclid than I did over the doctrine of transubstantiation.

My misery culminated in the preparation for the general confession extending over my whole life, that I had to make on being received. I had no conception of spiritual sin; because I had never stuck a knife into anyone, or got drunk, I was quite satisfied with myself. How furious Father F. got with me, how he bruised and broke me. Nothing astonished me more than the fact that he dwelt so briefly on the sins of the flesh, and so strongly on those of the spirit. Slowly, indeed, I came to comprehend how one might love publicans and sinners and loathe Pharisees and hypocrites.

At last I knew myself in a true light; at last real sorrow and contrition were mine, and I was able to go humbly and meekly to the Sacrament of Penance.

All bleeding and exhausted, I won my way into Holy Church—the Angel's Food was mine; the Holy Grail was found!

Chapter III

Calm after Stormy Seas

I WOULD not have others think that the entrance to Mother Church is always a fight—day after day I see weary sheep led gently within the fold ; on the other hand, I would not that my instruction and reception had been otherwise ; it was all the Lord's ordering, and I know now that not one difficulty but was necessary in my case. And I had no home opposition to test me ; when I told my father of the step I contemplated he replied characteristically :

" It is not worth while to change your ceremonial, child ; all religions are religious to those who know how to worship, and it is wiser to stick to

the country you are born in and the
church you are reared in, rather than
to fly to ills ye know not of."

But all the same, after I had been a
Catholic for about twelve months, he
one day kissed my forehead (a very
unusual caress with him) and re-
marked :

" Your religion seems to have made
you happier and better, child."

Father F. had been shocked at my
description of our family life ; at the
absence of deep affection, and the free-
dom with which we each went our
own way, without even consulting one
another. Under his direction I tried
to cultivate family affection and a
more intimate home circle ; but I was
not successful. My eldest sister was
now matron of a poor-law infirmary
in the north, and I went and spent a
week with her. She was a very capable
and cold person, and her callousness
in the presence of pain and death

made my soul shiver. She never thought of the patient's spiritual needs —they were mere bodies to her. There could be no possible working together between her and me. And yet I was longing to do real hard work for our Lord's sake. Like most converts I wanted to become a nun, and Father F. sent me down to the Italian Church and Hospital to see the work of the Sisters of St. Vincent de Paul ; but though I felt the keenest admiration I felt no vocation.

My second sister had married, and with her I was, strangely enough, much more in sympathy. The time of her engagement had coincided with my period of instruction, and I had listened one day whilst the others bantered Olive as to her reasons for liking her elderly and plain suitor.

" Because of his moustache," said Olive, and was greeted with roars of laughter. Then she raked up other reasons—she wanted to get away from us—four daughters living at home was absurd ; she wanted a home of her own ; and at last she said boldly :

" Because I love him, and love needs no reason."

Oh, how I wished Father F. could have heard her ! I knew that exactly as her love was an unreasoning impulse of the heart, so was my religion an unreasoning impulse of the soul. Both transcended all reason, both were divine gifts. And exactly as some people go through life without any knowledge of love, so many go through life without any knowledge of religion.

My eldest sister, in our then parlance, had no heart, she could not in the least understand Olive ; but Olive could not in the least understand me. I took her one day to Benediction at the Oratory, and she sat patiently through that most devotional service. And when she came out she said :

C

"But where does the congregation come in? There were no hymns and no sermon; nothing they could understand or take part in."

"But they *did* understand! They know, and I know, every word of that service by heart, and the meaning of every action of the priest—it is an act —a service of God—it is not for expanding the congregation's lungs, or tickling their intellect with interesting arguments on things in general!"

"Well, on the whole I prefer the Salvation Army,"* said Olive, and that ended my attempts to convert my family. This must have been the year '87, for I remember the jubilee bonfires twinkling from every hill on the 21st of June; also I remember going to see Sarah Bernhardt, and also hearing the late Lord Russell of Killowen—then Sir Charles Russell—speak on Home Rule. I mention these things

* The Army was not then popular.

merely to show that I was living in the
world, and even so much so that I can
remember details after twenty years.

In the year 1888 an old friend of
my father's died and left me, and each
of my sisters, £1000. I cannot quite
tell how the possession of this money
changed my view of the future ; I had
felt I ought to work with my hands—
to nurse—to visit the poor—but yet
that work repelled me, and there was
tugging at my heart a desire I could
not understand. I was so terribly
ignorant that I had no knowledge of
the lives of the contemplatives—I had
just heard of Saint Teresa, but that
was about all. I had such a terrible
lee-way to make up ! Remember I
had had no Catholic training as a child,
and I was always running up against
some fact which children had sucked
in with their mothers' milk, but which
was new and marvellous to me. Nothing can ever replace the deprivation of

not having had a Catholic upbringing,
and I think the born Catholic might
often be kinder to the sadly handi-
capped convert. I had joined one of
the sodalities of the Church, and at the
meetings made friends with a quiet,
elderly lady, who offered to lend me
books. From lives of the Saints she
led me gradually on to more mystical
literature, and then suggested I should
join a retreat to which she was going.
The retreat was held at the convent
of an order of " enclosed " nuns—or
nuns who never leave the grounds of
their convent. I spent a week there—
a week of silence, prayer, and meditation, with addresses three times a day
from a Jesuit priest. I was introduced
for the first time to the Exercises of
St. Ignatius—a whole new world was
opened up before me, and I knew at
once what that persistent pull on my
heart-strings meant. This was the
knowledge I craved ! The futility of

deeds—the power of thought—became patent to me—I wanted to do nothing else for the rest of my life but to seek God in prayer.

Before my old materialistic ideas had held me captive. I had tried to *do* things, and I had wanted to earn my way. Now I saw myself with what I considered a sufficiency for food and raiment, for the support of the outer life, and all this wonderful inner life opening out before me. I suppose that sounds an absurd estimate of £1000 to most ; but I knew how little it cost to keep a nun. Did not the Brussels nuns keep me for £30 a year ? Then my family had no need for me : his daughters being saved from fear of starvation, my father had given over saving, and he and my mother and two younger sisters lived very comfortably together on what he was earning. And his practice had improved enormously of late. I knew I had found my vocation, but I did not act hurriedly —I was well content to stay quietly at home and muse and read. My ignorance appalled me more and more. I was over twenty-one now, but I told my father what my wishes were, and asked his consent. We argued the matter out quietly; he said he was strongly against anyone taking a life vow, for we were all subject to change. I pointed out that Olive had taken a vow to love, honour, and obey a man for life, and that I thought it would be easier to keep a vow to serve God than a vow to serve a man. Finally he requested me to choose an order where he could see me at intervals, and where I should have an opportunity to change my mind at the end of my noviceship.

We settled amicably what I was to demand of the order I was to enter, and then off I went in search of the order! Again I could laugh at the

ignorance and self-sufficiency from
which I suffered. Soon I learnt it was
not for me to pick and choose, but to
sue humbly for admittance at the
heavenly gates. I had to prove to
my director that I had a vocation,
and then find a Rev. Mother willing
to receive and test me. At last, early
in 1889, after a brief postulancy, I was
received as a novice at a convent in
the Midlands.

Chapter IV

The Novice

THE ceremony of " clothing," or " taking the white veil," is a very picturesque one, and one to which the novice's near relations are always invited—whether they are Catholics or Protestants. The whole community comes in in procession, carrying lighted tapers, and in the middle are the new novices dressed as brides, and attended by bridesmaids. The priest is seated before the altar, and when the would-be novices kneel before him, he asks them :

" Quid petis ? " ("What wouldst thou ? ").

And they reply :

" Misericordiam Dei et vestram " ("God's mercy and yours.")

The priest then gives a brief exhortation on the rule and spirit of the order, and on what the religious life means, and the solemnity of the step about to be taken. He then blesses the habits and sprinkles them with holy water, and the novices retire and have their hair cut and put on the major part of the habit.

As they return the *Veni, Creator Spiritus* is sung ; the novices again kneel before the altar, and, with the help of the Mother Superior, the priest puts on their girdle and veil, bidding them receive them as symbols of purity and restraint. The *Te Deum* is then sung, a few prayers are said, and the priest sprinkles the novices with holy water and blesses them, and the religious ceremony is over. But there are generally further jubilations in the refectory, where a bridal cake and glasses of wine are dispensed, and the

Mother Superior kisses the new novices on each cheek.

My father and mother were both present at my clothing, and both lunched at the convent subsequently, and were allowed to see the grounds.

My father was informed that I should write home once a month, and that he was free to come and see me once in three months; and that he would be invited to be present at my profession should I be successful in the novitiate and be admitted to the order.

I found that day trying, and it seemed to me rather childish; but my two fellow-novices, who were younger, were very lively and full of enjoyment of the ceremony.

In the afternoon we were given a brief instruction by the Novice Mistress, and our time-tables, and were then sent to our cells, which we only left again that night for Benediction.

The convent was a square, uninteresting house enclosed in a large but ill-kept garden ; there was nothing beautiful about it but the chapel. My cell was an ordinary rather large bedroom, in which the scanty furniture looked somewhat forlorn ; the refectory was a square dining-room with French windows and a hideous mantelpiece of carved fruit. There was great lack of the picturesqueness and appropriateness of my school convent near Brussels. The time-table, which was put into my hands, ran as follows :

ORDO DIURNUS

Hora 5.   Surgitur.

  ,, $5\frac{1}{2}$.   Meditatio.

  ,, $6\frac{1}{2}$.   Examen meditationis in cubiculo.

  ,, $6\frac{3}{4}$.   Tempus liberum.

  ,,   7.   S.S. Missæ sacrificium.

  ,, $7\frac{1}{2}$.   Jentaculum.

  ,, $8\frac{1}{4}$.   Horæ minores.

  ,, $8\frac{3}{4}$.   Tempus liberum.

  ,,   9.   Laboro.

  ,, $10\frac{1}{4}$.   Visitatio Sanctissimi.

  ,, $10\frac{1}{2}$.   Lectio communis.

Hora 11¾. Examen conscientiæ generale.

,,   12.   Prandium.

,,   12½. Tempus liberum.

,,   2.   Vesperæ et Completorium.

,,   2½.   Studeo.

,,   4.   Matutinum et Laudes.

,,   4¾.   Meditatio.

,,   5¾.   Examen meditationis.

,,   6.   Cœna.

,,   6½.   Relaxtio animi.

,,   7½.   Benedictio con S.S.

,,   8.   Examen conscientiæ.

,,   8½.   Decubitus.

Beneath this minute dividing of the day were various *Notanda*, written in Latin, which pointed out where silence was to be maintained and so on. I was disappointed to find that the novices did not rise at midnight to say matins and lauds as the nuns did, and that, as a matter of fact, we saw but little of the eight or ten nuns of the convent, except on *festas*. The Rev. Mother spoke to each of us daily, and generally presided over the *Lectio communis*. Also, she sent for us one by one every now and then and questioned us on our progress. The meals were excellently served and the food was good ; very different, indeed, from the food in Belgium. For breakfast there was *café au lait* and large slices of bread and butter ; for dinner there was meat and vegetables and pudding ; for supper there was tea, and cold pudding, or boiled eggs. Of course, on fast days there was no meat, but there was fish or soup instead. During Advent and Lent those nuns who wished it went without butter, but this was not allowed to the novices. I have been asked specially to mention these points, and also to say that the beds were most comfortable, and there was a sufficiency of warm blankets for winter. As regards the habit, it was often rather hot in summer, but during twenty years I only remember once really suffering from it, and that was one Corpus Christi festival, when the sun on the black veil on my head was so hot I was afraid of sunstroke, and had to leave the procession between the first and second altars. One other point I am asked to mention : on Friday nights the nuns took the discipline in common. The discipline was a small scourge of whipcord—there were no steel points. The Rev. Mother or Novice Mistress knelt at a fald-stool at the end of the passage and recited aloud the *Miserere ;* the nuns knelt on the floor, each in their own cell, the doors being half open and the lights extinguished. They repeated the verses of the psalm alternately with the Rev. Mother, and struck themselves across the shoulders with such lightness or heaviness as they chose. Then was said—"Domine, non secundum peccata nostra facias nobis." ℞. "Neque secundum iniquitates nostras retribuas nobis." And then the prayer, "Deus, qui culpa offenderis, pœnitentia placaris, preces populi tui supplicantis propitius respice, et flagella tuæ iracundiæ, quæ pro peccatis nostris meremur, averte " —which shows so fully the meaning of this and other mortifications.

I might dwell long on our fasts and *festas*, but what probably the world can least understand is that it is not the seclusion, but the life in common which is the greatest penance. What would not I have given in those early days to be allowed to make my daily visit to the Blessed Sacrament alone! But I had always to kneel between the two other novices, and one of them invariably used the time to murmur her rosary. A lonely hermitage on a hill-top, combined with all the privileges of community life and frequent enjoyment of the sacraments, was the impossibility for which I sighed.

The novitiate is purposely made hard in many ways to thoroughly test the novices and turn back those of no vocation. But the actual teaching of our Novice Mistress was a great delight; she was a brilliant Greek and Latin scholar, and had a fair knowledge of Hebrew. She was of French descent, and her manner was always soft and gentle, though her rules were of iron. I had a great reverence and admiration for her, and often thought then that she was worthy of a larger sphere. Her lessons on the Psalms, on the beautiful Greek liturgy of St. John Chrysostom of the golden mouth, and above all her lessons on prayer, I shall never forget. Nothing is more difficult to teach than meditation and contemplation. I feel bound to try and offer one of her jewels, for if any can appreciate it aright, I believe it will open the gates of heaven for them, as it did for me. It seems to me more worth writing about than aught else in my life.

The subject of the meditation was love or charity, and the first prelude was picturing the red lamp that burns ever before the Blessed Sacrament and recalling the prayer in the mass, " May the Lord kindle in us the fire of His love, and the flame of everlasting charity." The symbolism of the sacred fire was to be dwelt on. The second prelude was the beautiful thirteenth Corinthians, which our Novice Mistress had taught us to read and repeat in the Greek.

Then for the Central Meditation we had written thus on a piece of paper :

1. The house and those therein.
2. The town and those therein.
3. Europe and those therein.
4. The whole world and those therein.
5. Other worlds—the universe.
6. Heaven and the Heavenly Host.
7. God.

We each knelt at our little praying-stools with bent heads and hidden eyes,

D

our mistress knelt facing us, with a small bell on her stool.

1. We were told to lift ourselves up in thought above the house in which we were and gaze down on all in it, and pour down on all our love and charity. " There must be no ill-feeling to anyone ; remember the lay sisters and the lodge-keeper ; do not forget the animals, the birds, the insects," murmured the voice of our instructress. Then, at the end of five minutes, a low stroke of the bell.

2. " Do not drop ; do not let your thoughts lower ! Higher, my children, higher ! Get well up above the town and look down on it. Let your love pour down especially on the Protestant churches. God, convert England ! Remember the children in the slums. See the men in the public-houses ; remember the Fathers in the Presbytery ; remember the prisoners in the prison." Again the bell rang.

3. " Higher, my children, higher ! all Europe lies below you now ! See our Holy Father at Rome ; see our fellow-religionists in Spain ; pour love on my poor atheistic countrymen, and love, more love, on the infidel Turk. Do not forget the poor Russian pea- sants.   And the animals—the dumb animals everywhere, and the beautiful flowers, pour down your love on all— all ! "   The bell rings.

4. " Higher, my children, higher ! Now the whole round world lies below you. The heathen ! the Indians ! the negroes ! Remember all our mission- aries at work—love the Chinese, love the Japanese. See all the sailors on the seas ; see the Arabs in the desert ; see Jerusalem upon its Holy Hill." The bell rings.

5. " Now look around you, children ; cast your eyes down no more. See all those other worlds—planets, stars, clusters, nebulæ. Thousands and thou-

sands that no man can number, but because God made them we can send our love radiating out to them all, we know that they are good, we know they shall be ours some day. How vast the universe! How vast is God!" The bell rings.

6. " Now look above, children ! Who are these ? Pierce the light! Lift your eyes to the saints and adore them. Do not fear. Blessed be God in His angels and in His saints. See the holy virgins and widows, the monks and hermits, the bishops and confessors, the apostles, the disciples—Holy Mary!" The bell rings.

7. " God."

Of late years I have never been able to go through with this meditation ; my thoughts always rush on without pause to the end. I know one of our novices was so bewildered as to whether her body really accompanied her soul above, that she tied herself to her stool with a piece of tape, and was greatly comforted at the end of the meditation to find the tape unbroken.

In seeking for the trials of those days the worst I can remember was the nun who tried to make me sing. Our small community was sadly in need of good voices, and I had a fair speaking voice, but alas, no ear for music. My efforts to take alto in the plainest chants broke down the patience of our organist ; and I got many a severe scolding from her. Still, I managed to pull through my twelve months in the novitiate with sufficient success to warrant the others in admitting me to the order. My father came down to say good-bye to me the day before my profession. He tried hard to make me say I was dissatisfied or repentant, and continually repeated that my place was still open for me at home. I think before he left he was convinced that all was well with me—and I was convinced that family affection had already begun to wane, and that my real home was the convent.

The ceremony of profession is more solemn than that of clothing ; though in the same spirit in which the novice asked for the habit, she now asks for admission to the order as a mercy to be received from God. The *Veni Creator* is sung, and the priest makes fuller interrogatory than in the former service, and then a lighted taper is given to the kneeling novice, and she repeats (in English) the form of profession : " To the honour of Almighty God "—undertaking to live henceforth according to the rule of the order. The black veil is then flung over the head and face of the nun, a crucifix put in her hand, and a ring on her finger, and she slips from her knees prostrate on the ground. A black cloth is held over her by four nuns, and the priest reads certain prayers from the burial service, as a sign that the nun is now dead to the world. Then, the nun rising, a joyful *Te Deum* is sung, and the blessing given. All the beautiful symbolism had come to mean much more to me by this time than at my clothing, and I felt a great wave of security and peace go over me when the veil was flung over my head. No one can have experienced greater happiness than was mine for the first few days after my profession. I was quite certain of my vocation, nor have I ever had any doubts since. · There must be many ways for many folk in this big world ; but for me there could only be the convent life—it was for that I was made.

Chapter V

The Enclosed Nun

SHORTLY after I was professed our house was amalgamated with another house of our order, thus making a larger community, and making the work much easier and pleasanter. A small community is very difficult to govern.

The special work of the community was holding retreats and instructing converts, so we had a large guest-house, and our own nuns had often to fall in with the arrangements made for those entrusted to our care. For many a long year I had nothing to do personally with our visitors—I was far too ignorant to take part in any in-structing—but I was kept busy in the housekeeping, and for two happy years as Sister Sacristan. All sorts of privileges were granted me gradually. I was allowed to take part in the night office, I was given a half-hour alone in the chapel every evening; I was admitted to the *Conferentia* once a week. Let me first state, however, that the nuns who rose at midnight slept half an hour later in the morning, and that the *tempus liberum* after dinner could always be used for sleep in one's cell if one so desired. Indeed, many of the old nuns always took a siesta, but I was so strong and vigorous it was my delight to spend this time in gardening. Once a month we had chapter, when the nuns, if they wished, made public confession of their sins against the rule—be it understood, of those sins only. The book of the rule was always read from at this chapter, and the Rev. Mother would call attention to such points as she thought needed impressing on the community. But there were other afternoons when the Rev. Mother would start and control a discussion on such subjects as, "Should a nun have knowledge of the world before she enters the convent, or is she happier if she passes straight from the school-room to the novitiate ? " " Is the contemplative life easier and pleasanter than the active life ? " " If an obligation of fidelity were substituted for the three vows, would perseverance in the religious life decrease ? "

Often these discussions were a serious distraction to me, and I begged to be excused them ; it was only very slowly that I got to see how valuable they were in letting the Rev. Mother judge of the state of those under her, and giving her opportunities to guide and help them along their path. There is much of a nun's life with which a Mother Superior can sympathise better than any Father Confessor; there are difficulties that arise, little gulfs between the ideal and the real; little tangles between good and evil, that are impossible of comprehension to those outside community life.

Some years later, when a period of spiritual dryness fell upon me, when meditation failed me, and even prayer seemed arid, I was glad indeed to put forward some of my temptations as hypothetical cases, and so let the love of the Rev. Mother shine on them and lighten their darkness. But in the darkest hour of my desolation it was from elsewhere that my help came; and if this record is to be of any use I had better try and remember what I can of Father Ambrose's instruction. The devil of *accidia* had got hold of me, and I had said that I could see no use in my life.

Father Ambrose told me I had not yet got over the influenza; that I was to go and ask the Rev. Mother for a glass of wine and a biscuit, and that he would talk to me in the afternoon. Instead of talking to me personally he gave an instruction to all the nuns over thirty, before Benediction.

By this time I had qualified to be present. He took as his text, " What profit hath he that worketh in that wherein he laboureth ? " and he dwelt on the spirit of *Cui Bono?* that, he said, oppressed the earth. He told of the author who said, like Solomon, why should I write ? it has all been said before, and said better: of the physician who found the practice of his youth changed, and the drugs he had been taught were useful now declared dangerous, and new methods being brought in in which he could not honestly believe. Of the mother who saw her children departing from the paths in which she had reared them ; of the sweeper sweeping the streets and the snow descending faster than he could sweep. What profit ? What is the use of it all ? Why is man born ? Why does he labour ? Why does he pray ? This is one of the dark phases of life every human being goes through between the ages of thirty and fifty ; and the religious is not left out. The monk says, oh that I had been a doctor to see the sick cured under my hand, then I should have seen of the labour of my soul and been satisfied ! And the nun, vowed to perpetual adoration, says, "Oh that I could scrub out one dirty room, clothe one naked child, that I might see and be satisfied." And the Sister of Charity goes down the same dirty street she has gone down for twenty years, and sees the same number of neglected children, and the same number of drunken men, and she says, " What is the use of it all ? If we rescue one child, two more seem to spring up in its place ! Oh that by prayer and contemplation I could increase the glory of God, rather than wasting my time in these hopeless slums!" And the preacher writhes in abasement and despondency as he sees his words bring forth no fruit. What profit? Oh, Lord, what profit? Well, it is just that there is no earthly system of profit and loss that can be carried into the things of God; the whole phase is one by which we learn the uselessness of all earthly things, and say with sad old Solomon, "Vanity of vanities!" The higher in worldly things we are when this phase comes on us, the more terrible the fall. Solomon, for instance, Napoleon, for instance. But great or small, we have all got to face this phase and go through with it; we have all got to learn the nothingness of things temporal—or else we are mindless idiots on whom thought is wasted. And we most of us come through on the other side chastened and gentler, willing to work without profit; the doctor ready to see his patients die if that be the will of God and able to perceive that that is the best thing for them; the politician willing to go on trying to make good laws for the public, though the many-headed beast turn on him with hissing; the nun able to lose herself in prayer once more and cling on to the hem of the garment of God; the preacher content to hesitate and suffer and be himself his only pupil. Why should the priest or the nun hope to get through life without periods of despondency more than other human beings? But owing to their glorious vocation, they ought to more swiftly conquer the temptation, the sooner arise from the mire. That was the tone of the instruction; it sent me back humbled and happy to my prayers. Such a little time afterwards —oh, such a little time!—and that happiness was taken from me, and I had to enter on the most difficult time of my life. I was elected Mother Superior. Now I found that I was seldom able to be present in chapel for the divine office ; that no matter what I was engaged in I was constantly being summoned to the parlour to see strangers and externes, and that I had the awful responsibility of the souls of those under me laid upon me. Once more I had to finger money and keep accounts ; worst of all, there was a farm connected with the convent, and I had to engage and dismiss the men, to buy and sell beasts and land. The chaplain stood manfully by me and aided my ignorance—when he could keep from laughing over my blunders, and the nuns all helped me in every way they could. Gradually I recovered my calm and got my hand on the work, but to this day I find it difficult to go gladly to the parlour, and I often groan when I hear the door-bell ring. But old age is before me, when this burden will be lifted from me. What happier picture is there than that of an aged nun? Surrounded by her fellows, passing peacefully through the well-ordered day, the beautiful services; the Holy Sacraments, there beside her; the waiting on the threshold for the call to come. We have ever before us the picture of Mother Margaret to make our thoughts of old age beautiful, and it is a picture I must try to write down.

E

Chapter VI

The Inner Life

NOW the real life of a nun is the inner life; the outer life is merely a routine the body learns to go through mechanically, and is of no importance. Progress in the spiritual life is our aim, and our goal is union with God.

I have given one of the simple meditations for novices, which may be taken as a first step in this life; but effort must be made to get beyond words and to arrive at contemplation.

It is here that the use of symbols comes in; when I cross myself before kneeling down to pray I, by that sign, put myself in the presence of God, make a confession of faith, and recall the whole meaning of that sign down two thousand years. Let me give a profane quotation in slightly altered form :

" Sick am I of idle words past all reconciling—
　　Words that weary and perplex and pander
　　　　and conceal,
　　Use the signs that cannot lie, for all their
　　　　sweet beguiling :
　　The language one need fathom not, but only
　　　　see and feel."

It is the pride of our order that its members say the divine office daily— that is " call unto the Lord seven times a day," at matins, lauds, sext, tierce, none, vespers, and compline. For this we meet together three times in chapel—at midnight, or the beginning of the new day, to say matins and lauds to the rising sun ; at eight to say sext, tierce, and none, which are called the minor hours ; and at two to say vespers and compline. These services consist largely of the old Hebrew Psalms, the admiration of which we share with Anglican, Presbyterian, Jewish, and other worshippers. There is always something fresh to be found in them, there is always some subject for thought, some help to be gained from this repeating of the office.

But also we meet in the chapel twice a day for an hour's silent meditation. At these times we do not necessarily sit in our stalls—we sit or kneel where we like, and we can use books or not as we like. A general outline for meditation for the week is always drawn up at chapter, and the nuns have to make note of it and carry the paper about with them. Also one conference each week is always devoted to the subject for meditation; but often a nun will simply remark that she is not following the given meditation, or more formally ask permission at chapter to follow her own line of thought. The Rev. Mother seldom interferes in these cases, unless she has reason to think a nun is becoming desultory or lazy in the inner life.

From eight o'clock at night, when we come out from Benediction, until eight o'clock the next morning, when we finish breakfast, no talking is allowed. Emergencies sometimes arise which make us very ingenious in the way of signs. For instance, the birds around are very tame, and the robins and sparrows like to come into the refectory and share our breakfast. Sometimes on a cold morning, when the window is shut, one very impertinent little robin will come and peck at it and peep in. Then a nun makes a little wordless request to the Rev. Mother for permission to open the window ; the window is opened and in comes Mr. Bobby, very much at home. The sparrows are quite content with dry bread, but Mr. Bobby likes butter, so if it is a fast day he will go down to the novices' end of the table, or go and perch himself on the plate of one of the elder nuns who is not allowed to fast. One of our old nuns is bedridden, and she has tamed some mice to come and share her breakfast, and her horror on a dark morning when a lay sister enters hurriedly—for fear the mice should be trodden on—makes her signs most vivid and expressive. But the silence on the whole is very beautiful and saving; there is much more trouble and danger in conducting or taking part in the conferences than in the great silence, or the hours of meditation.

It is such a lovely calm after Benediction—our only musical service of the day—to pass quietly to one's cell for the examination of conscience, and then to bed. And to pass in silence at midnight to chapel, say the office, and then pass in silence back. To rise in the morning for the hour's meditation in chapel, followed by the Mass and by thanksgiving; then the silent breakfast, taken standing, and no worldly word till at eight we take up our share of the day's outward work.

I am asked here to explain that the beautiful service of " Benediction " consists of a sung litany, of two hymns to be found in the English hymn-books under the titles " O Saving Victim," and " Down in Adoration Bending," and the making of the sign of the cross over the kneeling congregation by the priest, who raises high the Host enclosed in a monstrance. It is a service common in the evening and afternoon in Catholic churches, is very simple and devotional in character, and is one Protestants would do well to attend who desire an introduction to the rites of the Catholic Church. The priest says no words—merely makes the sign with the Host—a most blessed end to the day. This privilege is ours every evening except Fridays, and excepting the Wednesdays of Lent and Advent and the whole of Holy Week. On these evenings, instead of the music and lights and the exposition and blessing, we pass in silence to our dark cells and repeat the *Miserere* and take the discipline as described on page 46. Would it be well always to end the day on the note of praise and peace ? Are we to have no part in our Lord's Passion ? Are we to make no repentance for sin ? As a help to the inner life, as a step nearer towards union with God, the *Miserere* is as effective as Benediction. Be it understood that no nun need use the discipline unless she wishes ; that each uses it lightly or severely as she thinks best ; that the elder nuns and the novices are not allowed this mortification—they merely kneel on the floors of their cells and join in the prayer.

It is so difficult to try and explain to Protestants all we find in these symbolic services, but if it seems to us a means of showing our love to our Lord, and a means of partaking in the sufferings of humanity, and declaring our abhorrence of sin and our sorrow and regret at all the sins of the world, do we not do well to follow it ? In some sort of dim way we are trying to offer ourselves for others as well as to do penance for our own sins ; the desire at least is worthy and elevating, and the means of expressing it has been in use for nearly two thousand years. Any spiritual director of a religious house will acknowledge that the difficulty he finds is to moderate and control the voluntary mortifications of the inmates. Certainly I can say that I have never heard a nun grumble at this service, nor have I ever known one injured by the use of the discipline.

Another great aid to the inner life is the judicious use of books; we are justly proud of our library and of its careful classification. There are the books used for the instruction of converts, and for the instruction of their instructors; there are books on the history of our order and on the lives of its saints; there are books on ceremonial and church history. Our special glory is a collection of old books dealing with the history of the Catholic Church in England, and we have some valuable manuscripts with regard to the lives of the English martyrs. The use of certain books is restricted to those studying certain subjects. Diffuse reading is not encouraged. Our daily reading in common is taken either from the Gospels or the " Imitatione Christi "; and every nun can have the use of the books on mental prayer that have been selected as worthy of constant study. But

mere reading is of no use ; the actual
practice and following out of the rules
of such a book as " The Ascent of
Mount Carmel " may be helpful ; but
the greatest aid is obedience to a
spiritual director who is skilled in the
guidance of religious. We are subject
to frequent changes in our chaplains,
the same priest seldom stays more
than three to six years ; but we have
the advantage of constant visits from
other priests, and the bishop always
comes to us once a year. There is a
special retreat given for the nuns twice
a year, and also the day preceding the
annual renewal of our vows, we all
spend in retreat in our cells, saying the
office there, and having our meals
there, and only leaving them to go to
Mass. I have been trying to show the
many helps we have to the inner life,
and what the path we try to tread is,
and what the goal. To be always re-
collected, to be purged of all desire,

to reach "*Das nichts !* — the divine dark."

> "Oh rapture then to find
> The nothing vast and deep :
> Appeased the craving mind,
> The crying heart asleep."

But it is impossible to give articulate utterance to the things of the spirit.

The round of services of the Christian year, the constant commemoration of saints, leads us on and on along our road : Holy Church never leaves us alone—we are always being guided onward, given subject for meditation, given examples to remember and profit by. In its own way the inner life is as busy as the outer life ; and the days seem to fly past. Neither outwardly nor inwardly is there that " deadly monotony and routine " of which I hear we are accused.

Chapter VII

Outside the Gates

THREE times since I made my profession have I been without the gates; first in 1900, when we moved from our house in the Midlands to here; secondly in 1903, when I went to Rome to a general assembly of our order; thirdly in 1908, when I attended the Eucharistic Congress in London. On each occasion a special dispensation was necessary.

The first occasion was short and uneventful; but I did wish that, like St. Teresa, we could have driven all the way in a closed carriage, and kept our hours and said our office in it. A prison van would have suited nicely, and would have given such joy to the

Protestants, who will insist on regarding us as prisoners—and, I fear, as criminals !

But the trouble of moving was well repaid by the greater suitability of the convent we are now in. Only I hope I may never have to move again.

In 1903, by the direction of the Holy Father, two nuns from each province of our order met at the Mother House in Rome, to consider and vote on certain proposed modifications of our rule.

I was one of the nuns sent from England. I met my fellow-representative at Victoria, and we went via Newhaven to Paris, where we were housed for the night by the Sisters of Charity. We had only handbags with us, and we travelled second class, and said our office in the train. We went from Paris straight through to Rome, and spent three days there. Nuns were present from Canada and the United

States, and all parts ; one little nun from Brittany had never been in a railway train before. I never so felt the universality of the Catholic Church as at that conference. It was intensely interesting to file into choir and repeat the office, *not* with one's compatriots, but with nuns of many nations. Ah, when a Church is as big as the Catholic Church, it is mere common sense to have a common language ! It was a great amusement to me to try and talk Latin to the German and Spanish sisters ; and how we laughed as we invented Latin terms for modern inventions and for the things of everyday life.

We were received and blessed by the Holy Father, who confirmed the alterations in the rule, and we were taken over part of the Vatican and St. Peter's, and to visit the seven churches. It was a great uplifting to see Rome in its power—to meet so many notable people, but it was also to me a time of great distraction and brain weariness. It was with a very thankful heart that at the end of a week I found myself back in my own cell.

Then last year, by the wish of the Holy Father, our chaplain and two nuns attended the Eucharistic Congress at Westminster. I was again chosen, though I would rather that someone else had been sent. I had never seen Westminster Cathedral, and that filled me with wonder and joy, so did the great gathering, and the admirable tone of the papers. It seemed to me that when I entered Holy Church twenty years ago, it was a small and despised body in England, chiefly supported by Irish exiles and what were called " Newmanites."

To see people of all countries, religious of all orders, priests and laymen, aye, and women and men of title and repute, all gathering together in hundreds under the direction of a Papal Legate, was a wonderful sight. There were Dominicans and Franciscans, Benedictines and Carmelites, all moving about with as much assurance as though they were in Rome. I shall never forget the sight of High Mass in the Cathedral. The cardinals and bishops, the canons and premonstratensians, the rows and rows of clergy and of religious. And another thing which lifted my soul and enlarged my heart was the Greek Mass—the extra Eastern touches of it, and the beautiful chants ever breaking into the familiar *Kyrie Eleison!* It made the bond of brotherhood between East and West so very close; it made the dream of the Reunion of Christendom rise once more before our eyes.

On the last day of the Congress—a Sunday—our chaplain could not go up to London—he had too many duties to attend to, nor was it possible for

F

myself and my fellow-nun to go up in the morning. But we were very anxious to go up for the afternoon Benediction, and though the chaplain could not go, we two nuns started off alone. We had not made due allowance for the infrequency of Sunday trains, and when we arrived near the Cathedral we found the whole street blocked. We tried to force our way along, and showed our tickets, but though the police were very kind we could not get far, and soon found ourselves completely hemmed in. Then some ladies at a window behind leant out and called to us, and asked us would we like to come in and go on the roof of the house—that from there we should see well if the height would not frighten us. We accepted, and they came out and helped us in ; we were taken up in a lift to the top of the house, and then up a ladder, and we found ourselves on a long flat roof

extending right along directly opposite
the Cathedral. There was scarcely anyone there, except a photographer, and
two or three people from the Catholic
Association down below. Indeed, it
would not have been safe for anyone
who suffered from giddiness. We
looked down on the great crowd and
saw one or two rushes made, and
realised that all were not friendly.
For the first time we heard that the
Host was not to be carried. I need
not describe the procession—it is all
too recent—nor how the Papal Legate
came out on the roof of the porch of
the Cathedral to where a temporary
altar had been fitted up and, ap-
proaching to the edge, gave Benediction
over that vast crowd. Then passing
to another altar to the west, gave
Benediction there. The Blessing of
England ! We were exactly on a level
with the temporary altars, and could
hear across the street every word of

the prayer as Cardinal Vannutelli said it. And from the street below, led by the band, surged up the *Tantum Ergo* sung by all that mighty crowd. Why I dwell on this scene is because it showed to me the marvellous advance of Holy Church in twenty years—that huge Cathedral, that mighty crowd! Down below I could see the tall figure of Father F. of the Guild of Ransom, controlling and directing his guides, and it seemed to me that the prayer, " God, convert England," was indeed being answered. What I hope and pray for now, is that I may live another twenty years, if it is the Divine Will, and see a like progress.

Never again, I trust, will my enclosure be broken. Even after the stirring times of the Congress, when I got back to my cell, I was always doubtful whether it was well to have gone or not. So far as my own soul was concerned I am sure it was not, but I hope that possibly these experiences may make me more competent in dealing with novices and postulants, more sympathetic in appreciating the temptations and trials of the laity.

Chapter VIII

The Outward Life

THE outward life consists of work and play—yes, really there is play; indeed, two of the days of the year are always " play days," and sometimes others are added. By old custom, on the *festa* of the Rev. Mother the nuns always get up some little concert or entertainment, and after dinner cake and wine are always served round to all. Also the refectory is decorated, and except for the office hours, the time-table is not strictly adhered to.

Then, again by old custom, on Christmas Day, after the third Mass, the nuns and lay sisters meet together in the Chapter House and elect a

Rev. Mother and Novice Mistress of Play ; it being immediately the duty of the real Rev. Mother and Novice Mistress to kneel and kiss the scapular of the Play officials and undertake to submit to their decrees. Then the Play Mother and the Play Mistress proceed to plan the revels, which are kept up until Benediction. One of the games always indulged in is "The Queen Bee"—but I needn't further describe our frivolities. It is nearly always part of the fun to make lay sisters act the part of the Play officials. The place and importance of the lay sisters in convents is seldom properly understood. We have to draw most of them from the small farmer class in Ireland, and we seldom can get as many as we need. They bring no dowry. In the novitiate their training is much the same as that of the choir novices, except that during the hours of study they go down to the kitchen and get practical instruction there. Instead of the Divine Office, they say the Little Office of Our Lady—which does not vary with the season—and they therefore do not rise at midnight for matins and lauds. They do all the house-work and cooking (save that each nun keeps her own cell) and have the charge of the poultry and dairy. They are many of them of wonderfully holy and simple nature. They are, of course, kept through their old age, and tended with care and respect. Ladies by birth and bringing dowries have been known to enter our order as lay sisters, finding in the more humble position greater help towards the spiritual life. The lay sisters take their dinner and supper at the same table as the choir sisters, sitting just above the novices; but their breakfast they sit down to in the kitchen, and it is a more substantial meal than that provided for the choir sisters.

There is one peculiarity about the English lay sister that always amuses me, and that is her reverence for a " Sunday dinner." I have found it impossible to keep my lay sisters content unless they had roast beef and Yorkshire pudding every Sunday ! The concession about the breakfast is also one to insular custom ; our choir sisters are not all English, and those that are English have mostly had some experience on the Continent, so that coffee and rolls for breakfast all the year round does not strike them as a perpetual fast. As for the standing during this brief meal, it is rather a relief, for we spend many hours kneeling or sitting in chapel. Also it allows each nun when she has finished to make her bow to the Rev. Mother, her genuflexion to the crucifix, and to hurry off to the cleaning of her cell. That is the way the day's work begins for each ; afterwards the duties are divided according to arrangement ; it needs the full time of two nuns to attend to the chapel, and even then on feasts the help of lay sisters or novices has to be begged. One nun gives out the stores and superintends the domestic arrangements ; another has charge of the general correspondence, which often runs to twenty or thirty letters in a day. This is due to the number of ladies we come across through our special retreat work—it is that work I must now try to describe. The retreats go on nearly all the year round, with a pause before Lent and Advent. During the summer holidays we have special retreats for teachers and other workers who are only free then. Sometimes we have retreats for other religious, who lead the active life, and whose own convents are not suitable ; sometimes we have retreats for factory girls, or Children of Mary from poor London parishes. Our guest-house has twenty small bedrooms, but during the summer, by using an old coach-house for our lay staff, we can, at a pinch, put up forty or fifty guests. It depends on whether each guest has to have a separate room. The retreats for workers generally last three days ; those for non-workers last a week. The chaplain sometimes conducts the smaller retreats, but never the larger ones, as the strain would be too much for him ; for the longer retreats some priest comes down from London and stays in the chaplain's house. Now the mere domestic service for these constantly changing parties is great, and then there is the correspondence, and many of those who come keep up a correspondence with us all the year round. In this way, though we are enclosed, we are kept much—I doubt too much—in touch with the world. Each guest has to be visited daily by a nun for ten minutes, during which time she must do all the talking she is allowed during twenty-four hours! We often have neurotic women sent to us to whom silence seems impossible; they will make remarks at table, they will greet anyone they meet in the passages, and they will send for the Guest Mistress to complain about the heat or the cold! One has to choose the Guest Mistress and her assistant nuns with the greatest discretion. Those in retreat attend 7 o'clock Mass, take their meals in the guest-house, are in the chapel for instruction from 9–10, 1.30–2.30, 6–7, and are present at Benediction at 7.30. From 11–12 they walk in one part of the garden if it is fine, or in the cloisters if it is wet; the rest of the time they spend in their own rooms. When we have converts for instruction they generally keep the time-table of the retreat, if there is one in progress, but also have lessons

on the Catechism, Church history,
ceremonial, and so on, from two or
three of the nuns who have been
specially trained as teachers. They
also have a select library, from which
they can take books to read, and they
have to write papers, etc. A convert
generally stays with us for at least
two weeks ; of necessity she sees more
of the nuns than others do, and gets
to know them. The result is that we
are the frequent recipients of gifts of
all sorts and kinds ; that little dainties
for *festas* are always in the store cup-
board, and that we are enabled to
send to a poor London mission a large
number of silver crucifixes, valuable
rosaries, books, medals, etc., which are
sent to us, but which our rule does not
allow us to possess. I have always a
remembrance of the one or two crowded
cells I saw in Brussels, and have fought
against any relaxation of our rule in
this respect. But if any of our friends

ever think that our vow of poverty makes it impossible for us to have a "merry Christmas," we report quite gravely that on one Christmas Eve the postal van drove up with twenty-four parcels !

Then, in such a large establishment, there is a great deal of needlework to do ; in our work-room we make all our own habits, and we make a good many vestments for the chapel. The personal mending is chiefly done during the conferences and the common reading. Again, the laundry is very heavy work—I am often sorry for the lay sisters who spend so many hours standing ironing. One of the strongest choir sisters is always put over this department, and she actually does part of the very skilled starching and ironing necessary for getting up the veils, altar-cloths, etc.

It seems unnecessary to enumerate all the various occupations of the sisters—the organist, the infirmarian, and so on : we try to avoid haste and worry, but the place is always like a bee-hive, all alive and busy, and time never hangs heavily on our hands.

Chapter IX

Mother Margaret

NO picture of our life would be true without an account of Mother Margaret. She is seventy-three years of age, and has been invalided for over ten years by rheumatism. A special cell has been constructed for her with a window that looks into the chapel. To this window she is lifted every morning for Mass, and it is opened always when we say the office, and for the hours of meditation. For Mother Margaret insists on keeping the rule to the fullest extent of her power. She has suffered much, but her spirit is indomitable, and sometimes we think we have a future saint in our midst. Certainly we have had proof of the peculiar efficacy of Mother Margaret's prayers, and we are all constantly begging for her help in this direction.

" Pray for yourself," she generally answers. " I am going to pray for those who never pray."

One petition of hers has yet to be granted ; we have a Protestant doctor who has been very kind to Mother, and she in return would like to bring him into the Church.

" I do like to bring doctors to God," she says, and then she proceeds to count up all the medical men and women, from Dr. Agnes Maclaren downwards, who have been converts, and proceeds to pray for more.

One thing Mother missed when she was first invalided, and that was the birds who come to the refectory ; it was chiefly she who tamed them in the first instance. Then one morning she saw a mouse in her cell. " I am not

G

exactly a youthful David, I can't sling stones, but I can throw crumbs. So I tempted him gradually nearer and nearer "—as she talks the mice are running across the bed! Several of the nuns do not like the mice at all, are half afraid of them, and once the poor little beasts nearly upset the harmony of the convent. Mother had to have an operation, and the doctor brought along a Protestant nurse, and the nurse objected very strongly to the mice. I sent the nurse downstairs and told Mother I would telegraph to town for a Catholic nurse. "No; perhaps I am getting too fond of them—and the surgeon will be here in a few hours now. She must be allowed to catch them—if she can!" I sent the nurse back, and I don't know what happened, but the mice were not harmed. And when the nurse left after a few days, I saw her kneel and kiss the hem of Mother's sleeve! For we nuns have fallen into the way of doing this on entering and leaving Mother's cell ; at first she objected, then said, " Well, let it be the habit you reverence, and it will do you good ; there is not enough humility amongst us, I doubt."

Even Monsignor falls into this custom. Only once a year are the nuns supposed to " tell tales "—the rest of the time they must try and suppress all grumbling about one another. But once a year we have a " visitor," a dignitary of the Church, and he sees each nun alone in the parlour, and to him any complaints about the community should be made.

" The nuns of this convent are all angels," he said last time to Mother Margaret ; " I can't get them to grumble about one another at all."

" I know," said dear Mother, with a twinkle in her eyes. " I think even Satan has given up tempting them. I had a dream the other night, Monsignor. I dreamt Satan thought he would make a last attempt on Sister Celeste—he thought the nun who had to do with the guests might have a vulnerable point somewhere. So he dressed up and went and knocked at the door. And Sister Celeste opened it, and directly she saw him she knew him and cried out, " I knew you would repent some day ! Come in, *do*, dear, and let me see what I can do for you." And Satan turned tail and fled, and we've none of us seen him since ! "

Dr. Thomas sometimes brings Mother flowers ; but she always sends them down to the chapel. She prefers her cell in its absolute simplicity, with no ornament save the little wooden crucifix common to every cell.

" I do like St. John of the Cross on images and oratories," she says. "And I need to remember him, for when I was young I was much tempted by outward and visible things in religion. I

wanted to give some silly jewellery to
deck our Lady's statue !   Now I have
all I want in that sanctuary lamp
which I can see burning night and
day, and saying all I cannot say.   I
am like the old fisherman who couldn't
remember his prayers, so had them
written out for him, and pinned them
over his bed, and then just jerked his
thumb at them night and morning and
said, " Thim's my sentiments, O Lord ! '
So now, when I am too ill for thought
or prayer, I just look at the little red
lamp and say, ' Thim's my sentiments,
O Lord ! ' "

That is the way dear Mother puts
it ; but often she lies with closed eyes
and folded hands, on her bed, hour
after hour, simply wrapped away in
prayer.   When we look in and see her
thus we always leave her alone.

At Mass on Sunday mornings, and
on first Fridays, a little procession goes
up to Mother's room—first a nun

ringing a bell, then two nuns carrying tapers, then the priest carrying the Host; all kneel as the procession passes.

Could old age possibly be more beautiful than this? "It lacks human affection," the secular may say. It does, deliberately. A new novice will sometimes want to pour out her girlish enthusiasm on Mother.

"I do not want human affection," says the quiet, vibrant voice; "it is a distraction and a hindrance. And you have to give your whole heart to our Lord—turn away from the creatures, child, and love only the Creator. There should be no individual affection in a convent; if a nun loves one of her companions more than the rest, she spoils the spirit of community life."

When I told Mother Margaret about the request for a written account of our life as some sort of an answer to various slanders on convents, she said, "Well, *you* can apologise* for being a nun if you like; *I* am proud of it."

"But, dear Mother, we are all afraid that laws may be passed enabling seculars to inspect our convents and alter our rules if these stories of cruelty and oppression are unanswered."

"Let them inspect the 'happy homes of England,'" says Mother Margaret, "if they want to unearth scandals. We can most of us remember cruelty and oppression in our earthly homes; for myself, I have never known any convent scandals."

All postulants are put to wait on Mother Margaret, for she tries them as by fire, and her standard of moral worth is extremely high.

"Only the very best women are fit for the service of God; we should not

* In the original title—which was somewhat lengthy—the word "Apologia" was used.

allow our convent to be filled with the world's failures."

"But, dear Mother, she is very deaf and that has made her depressed."

"If she were a good woman she would have rejoiced in the deafness. Why, it is half-way to divine locutions to have the sounds of the world shut out so as to be able to hear inwardly. Depressed indeed! I have found her a grumbler against God and I shall vote against her."

Nor does the conceited postulant, secure in her own learning, fare any better with dear Mother; one ended up a long tale of her own persecutions at home with the phrase, "But I am sure I was right to be firm; we must stand up for our Lord, mustn't we, Mother?"

"If you are sure you were right, why ask me? Why come into a convent to learn humility and obedience? *I* believe our Lord can stand up for

Himself and needs neither your aid nor mine."

But for the shy and timid Mother is all encouragement :

" She has a vocation, that new postulant of yours ; she cleaned out my cell this morning without even once speaking."

" But she made enough noise other-wise, I expect, Mother. Didn't she knock over everything she touched ? "

" She is clumsy at present ; she is evidently quite unused to handling a broom. But she didn't tell me so—as though I had no eyes of my own ! And she didn't apologise ; she just did her best ; and then before she went looked at me half pleadingly, half humorously, and asked, would I tell her if there was anything she had left undone she ought to have done. I said, ' Yes, doubtless ; but not with regard to me or my cell,' and she smiled and went away. I like her, she will make a good nun—and a beautiful one, too."

It is largely due to Mother Margaret's clearness of vision and firmness of purpose that our standard has been kept so high ; no postulant can be received as a novice without a two-thirds vote of the community ; and no novice can be professed except with the unanimous consent of the community ; so that really Mother Margaret's vote is all-important—and the novices know it ! And the example of this clever, devout woman, always cheerful, always strong in mind however feeble in body, is good for us all. The burden of being laid aside must be far harder to her than to many others, but there are never any repinings nor excuses ; no apologies that she is a trouble to us ; no longings for death. She is absolutely happy under the Divine Will— and that is as near perfection as a nun may well get.

Chapter X

Looking Back

DO nuns ever long to return to the world ? One can only speak from one's own experience, and during my twenty years of convent life I have never known a nun who wanted to return to what are called the *pleasures* of the world. Our own joys are so far greater and more glorious. But the temptations of doubt and despondency come to most at times, and it is particularly those who have entered religion late in life who are tempted to look back and doubt whether they took the right step. Sometimes it is the thought of relations or friends in trouble ; sometimes the thought of a child left motherless ; sometimes the thought of one's own unworthiness and lack of progress in the spiritual life. I know this chiefly because nuns have said at the conference on whether an obligation of fidelity instead of the three vows would decrease persistence in the religious life, that they were glad indeed that their vows had held them so firmly through these times of gloom, and that any relaxation would be a great mistake. To suppose that a nun is never tempted is to suppose she does not toil heavenward. But the nun who enters religion early is least tempted with worldly thoughts ; memory can play her fewer tricks, Satan cannot suggest so many doubts. I know one of our nuns ever bitterly regrets that she was persuaded to " go round the world " before becoming a postulant. The evil she saw often comes between her and her vision of God. But to describe the spiritual combat of the religious is impossible ;

there are a few practical points I can put forward instead.

Quite half our postulants leave, either because they find our life impossible, or because we find them unsuited to the life—i.e. they have no " vocation." And the postulants sometimes grumble about material things, and long for worldly luxuries. One of our novices left after nine months by mutual consent—she found the life too hard, in her estimation. One of our novices had to leave on account of health—and she was heart-broken at going. One novice was refused on account of a violent temper—amounting almost to a physical infirmity. She was kept in the novitiate eighteen months, but it really seemed impossible for her to gain control over these sudden bursts of ill-feeling. She also wept bitterly, and we were all sorry for her.

No nun has ever left our convent,

though up to seven years from the time of her entrance it is possible for her to do so by mutual consent and by special dispensation from her vows.

We have received one nun who had left the convent in which she was professed. I was summoned to the parlour one day and there found Father B. and a forlorn-looking little woman, with a funny fashionable hat stuck on the top of a close-cropped head. It seemed that she had passed from the schoolroom into a teaching order, and all had gone well for three or four years, except that she found the girls difficult to manage, and that worried her. Then she had come in for some money, and her solicitor had had to have several interviews with her. It was not an enclosed order, and there was no difficulty about the interviews ; another nun was always present, but she sat some way off, and never noticed anything. Probably nothing was said, but written suggestions were given to the nun to read ; be that as it may, one day the solicitor suddenly took the nun by the arm and hurried her away to his carriage—the flight being covered by the clerk, who was there nominally to witness signatures. How far the nun consented or had agreed I do not know ; but the solicitor—who was a Protestant—soon found out that he had made a mistake. His strange little guest shrank from everything he wanted her to do. She clung to her habit, she hated meeting people, she was so shy and miserable she would hardly speak.

The solicitor had entered into a correspondence with the Provincial of the order, who said the only thing to be done was to dispense the nun from her vows and she must return her habit and ring. The solicitor was trying to keep the nun away from all priests, but on Sunday the poor girl insisted on going to Mass, and as she consented to put on worldly things to go in, this was granted. Then one day she fled into the sacristy and begged the priest there to take her back to the convent. Her own order would not receive her again, holding she had proved unsuitable for the life, and so Father B. brought her to us to see what could be done. She was thoroughly ill by this time, and we put her in the guest-house under gentle Sister Celeste, and we let the solicitor see her as often as he desired. He admitted, ruefully, that she was quite unfitted for the world, and that it was the only case he had ever known of a nun running back to a convent. We told him it was the first case we had ever known of a nun running away. He owned he had acted unwisely and arbitrarily, and that it was all his fault; he became quite amiable when he saw his client growing happier and stronger, and when he found that her late convent intended to make no claim on her money, and that we only asked a fraction of her fortune as a dowry. After a year in the guest-house she became a postulant—and after another year in that position, was allowed our habit, and renewed her vows when we did; the dispensation had not been proceeded with. She is one of the humblest and happiest nuns in the convent, with a great gift for contemplation, and a true love of silence. I am sure she never looks back on her few weeks in the world without a shudder. But she looks forward with the sweetest security; her terrible fall having been pardoned, she rests on God's love with the most perfect trust, and all her timidity is a thing of the past. I was pleased not long since in the parlour to hear her tell her solicitor that she had been far more a prisoner with him than ever in a convent.

H

" What, with that grille between us ? " he asked.

" Yes," she answered laughingly. " I need that grille to protect me from you."

The solicitor is an older and a wiser man now. I don't think he will ever abduct a nun from a convent again.

We have another nun who commenced her life in religion in another order ; she was a novice with the Poor Claires, and her health broke down and she had to leave. Now the Poor Claires go barefoot—no stockings, no sandals even ; they never eat meat ; they have no lay sisters, so that they have to do all the domestic work, and yet they say the Divine Office. This really is a hard novitiate, and no wonder there are some failures. This little novice went to friends at Bournemouth for the winter, and then came to us as a guest for a time. The only thing that drew her to us was that we

said the Divine Office and were enclosed; she longed for a far stricter
rule than ours, and greater mortifications.

At last she came to see that for her
the greatest mortification was to eat
meat and wear shoes, and she asked
to be received into our novitiate. She
is only perfectly happy when she is
sent to wait on some of our rudest and
most neurotic guests; it is almost a
relief to me sometimes when a piece of
very difficult work arises, for I know
how happy Sister Agnes will be when
I put her on to it. She never looks
back to regret the world, but only to
regret the greater strictness of her
previous cloister.

A chief part of the work of a Superior
is to watch over and help her nuns
when she notes them suffering from
spiritual ills, such as *accidia* or dryness,
or such physical ills as headache or in-
digestion.

Dispensations as regards fastings or hours may be " presumed," and a nun allowed to make a retreat in her cell, if her troubles are spiritual; or to pin up her habit and go and work in the hay field if her troubles are physical. Fruits and soups for those of weak digestion can also be provided, but as a rule a change of occupation is the best cure for depression. With a little common sense and care on the part of the Superior there ought never to be trouble with " looking backwards " if the novices are well and discreetly tested before being received. But St. Teresa says, and I have heard it from other convents, that one nun of doubtful " vocation " will upset a whole community of devout women and do untold mischief. The only thing to do in such a case is to get rid of the offender as soon as possible. No matter at what cost, get her a dispensation, and get rid of her. To us a nun who breaks her vows is looked on with the same horror as the world regards an unfaithful wife—nay, our disgust and shrinking is probably far greater, for is it not a worse sin for a nun to run away from her heavenly Spouse than for a wife to run away from her earthly husband ? Either is bad enough, both are best not spoken about more than is necessary, the subject is too horrible.

Chapter XI

The Centre of All

MANY of the enclosed orders are devoted to the perpetual adoration of the Blessed Sacrament. That privilege is not ours; but we have the Host ever reserved in our chapel, and that is the centre of our spiritual life. Our Beloved is ever with us.

Cardinal Manning says : " The presence of the Incarnate Word in the Blessed Sacrament is the basis and the centre of an order of divine facts and operations in the world. They spring from it, rest upon it, and are united to it, so that where the Blessed Sacrament is, they are—where it is not, they cannot be."

I know this is difficult of comprehension to the Protestant who does not believe in the Real Presence, but unless this is understood the life of the religious is not understood. For myself, though I have learned many arguments, I have no use for them.

" No other proof I ask, dear Lord,
    Than Thine own words of yore :
  ' This is My Body, this My Blood '—
    Oh, who could wish for more ? "

Faith came to me suddenly, and the great gift of a vocation was granted to me, and I entered on my years of prayer, and " He is a rewarder of them that diligently seek Him."

In the world of art or science it is recognised that concentration and persistence alone produce great results. We believe that the gift of contemplation is as much a rare and undeserved grace from God as is the gift of painting, sculpture, music, or poetry. But as the artist has to be trained and the musician has to practise, so must the nun be taught and must persevere in the course of prayer if she is to attain to " the secret of the Lord."

As in the world you may hear men and women say they are glad they have had their living to earn, because it helped to keep them constant and diligent in their work, so I look back and delight in our vows and our rule. Possibly I might have squandered, wasted, spoiled, mutilated this generous gift of seeing and hearing inwardly which God has bestowed on me, had I not come to live under the steady radiance of the Blessed Sacrament, with all distractions put aside and all possibility of the superficial dabbling in many things been taken from me. How terrible the worldly life of trifles and little things seems to those who are engaged with eternal truths. And without the life of the cloister to hold safe the mystical secret through ages of

revolution and materialism, what knowledge would have been lost ! Wave
after wave of tribulation goes over
Holy Church—here the murder of her
priests, there the heresy of her people ;
but always some little band in silence
and seclusion guard the Sacred Fire—
the Holy Water—the Living Bread.
So that all down the ages Christ has
never left us—our Beloved has always
been with us. Never has the chain
been broken, never has the secret been
lost. Thousands and thousands have
died—thousands and thousands have
lived with no other thought than to
keep intact this precious inheritance.
And how is it possible for those who
are without the gates to comprehend
all that this means to us ? To grasp
the height and the depth of the life
of a religious ?

Someone has said that the Catholic
Church is like a great cathedral with
beautiful windows of coloured glass ;

and that it is only from within that these windows and colours can be seen and appreciated. Remembering my youth and my conception of a church merely as a society, and of prayer merely as a repeating of words, and of Communion merely as a form of remembrance, I tremble to think how great would have been my desolation had I not managed to stumble over the threshold of the great cathedral, and into the presence of my Spouse and King. My ignorance was great, yet slowly, year by year, knowledge increased and the vision enlarged. It is difficult to think that seculars pity us instead of envying us; yet I can understand that to be a professed nun and not to have a vocation would be too terrible to be borne; the only thing to do would be to secure a dispensation and retire.

In our convent there is Exposition of the Blessed Sacrament all day on the first Friday of every month, on the first Sunday in October, and on the last day of the year. Also twice a year we have the " Forty Hours "—or Exposition for two days and nights. These are our great times of bliss. During Exposition at least sixteen candles are kept burning, and at least two watchers kneel below the altar. These hours of watching through the night are very beautiful. As the forty hours close at one church they open at another, so that somewhere the Blessed Sacrament is ever being publicly adored. The Blessed Benedict Labré was known in Rome as the " Saint of the Forty Hours " because he passed from one church to another to worship and adore. Only a poor beggar man who prayed, who never spoke or wrote or gathered followers or founded an order—yet Mother Church counts him Blessed— sees the Saint in him, for his devotion to the Blessed Sacrament. The secret is there somewhere for those who have eyes to see it ; for me it shows less in any treatise or book of doctrine than in that most common of Catholic hymns :

" Sweet Sacrament divine
Hid in Thy earthly home ;
Lo ! round Thy lowly shrine
With suppliant hearts we come.
Sweet light so shine on us, we pray,
That earthly joys may fade away,
Sweet Sacrament divine."

THE END

CPSIA information can be obtained at www.ICGtesting.com
Printed in the USA
BVOW051851020713

324928BV00003B/59/P

9 781276 387217